30秒でできる！
47
都道府県紹介
おもてなしの英会話

安河内哲也＝監修

JN251576

IBC

IBC PUBLISHING

本書の音声ダウンロードは
弊社ホームページから！

www.ibcpub.co.jp/shokai/

装幀 = 斉藤 啓

ようこそ！ ニッポンおもてなし列島へ！

　訪日外国人の数が増え続けています。また、訪問先もかつての
おきまりの観光地から、日本各地津々浦々へと拡大しています。
最近では、地方都市でも海外からの観光客を見かけることが大変
多くなりました。英語でのおもてなしは、都市部に住む一部の人
たちだけの問題ではなく、日本中の人々の課題になりつつあります。

　さて、皆さんは、自分の住む地域や名所のこと、また、自分の
住む都道府県や他の都道府県のことを英語で紹介することができ
ますか？　意外と内容が思いつかないのではないでしょうか？

　私自身も、英語以前に我が国、日本のことをもっと学ぶことが、
多くの外国人を日本に迎えるに当たって重要だと痛感しています。

　本書には、短く簡単な英語で、日本の観光地や各都道府県の特
徴を説明するための英語が収録されています。日本は本当に文化
資源にあふれた国ですから、細かいところまで説明し始めるときり
がありません。そこで、本書では、約30秒以内で各項目を説明す
るためのシンプルな英語を使用することを目標としています。

　まずは、自分の住む都道府県や自分に関連がある場所から、ガ
イドの練習をしてみましょう。その後は、私たちの国の形を学びな
がら、全都道府県制覇を狙いましょう！　ダウンロードできるネイ
ティブの音声を利用して耳から学んだり、発音練習をしたりする
こともおすすめします。

　国際イベントを成功させるためにも、私たちひとりひとりがおも
てなし大使です。英語は使うために学ぶものですから、ぜひ、本
書で学んだ内容を実際にどんどん使ってみてくださいね！

安河内哲也

目次

Contents

第6章　近畿 143

第8章　中国 169

第1章

基本構文

1 場所

有名な場所を解説するために便利な表現をみてみましょう。歌舞伎座や京都の市場として有名な錦小路を取りあげていますが、それらの代わりに自分が解説したい場所を当てはめて練習をしてみるといいでしょう。特に便利な表現は太字にしてあるので参考にしてください。

▶ 歌舞伎座は歌舞伎**の本拠地**です。

▶ 歌舞伎座は地下鉄東銀座駅の**近くにあります**。

▶ 歌舞伎座は銀座の中心から**歩いて**7分ほどです。

▶ 錦小路は京都**の中心に**あります。

▶ 京都に行くなら、錦小路に行くのを**忘れないで**ください。

▶ 錦小路は、外国人**に**とても人気があります。

Location

▶ The Kabuki-za Theater is **the home of** kabuki.

▶ The Kabuki-za Theater **is located near** Higashi-ginza Subway Station.

▶ The Kabuki-za Theater is located seven minutes **on foot** from the center of Ginza.

▶ Nishiki-koji is located **in the center of** Kyoto.

▶ **Don't forget** to visit Nishiki-koji when you go to Kyoto.

▶ Nishiki-koji is very popular **among** foreigners.

▶ 錦小路は、あらゆる種類の昔ながらの食べ物が見つかる市場**のようなところ**です。

▶ 桂離宮に**行くと**、伝統的な洗練された建築物と美しい庭を**見ることができます**。

▶ 桂離宮を**見るには**、**予約**が必要です。予約は京都観光センターでもできます。

▶ 京都観光センターは、京都駅ビルの2階に**あります**。

▶ 京都観光センター**の電話番号**は、075-343-0548 です。

▶ Nishiki-koji is a marketplace **where** you can find many kinds of traditional foods.

▶ **If you visit** Katsura Rikyu, **you can see** sophisticated traditional architecture and a beautiful garden.

▶ **To see** Katsura Rikyu, you need to **have a reservation**. You can make one through the Kyoto Tourist Information Center.

▶ The Kyoto Tourist Information Center **is located on** the second floor of the Kyoto Station Building.

▶ **The telephone number of** the Kyoto Tourist Information Center is 075-343-0548.

ここでは奈良国立博物館を例にとって、施設の情報をいかにして伝えればよいかを解説しています。博物館や美術館、あるいはお寺の参観情報など様々なケースに応用できるはずです。

▶ 奈良国立博物館は、日本の古代史**を学ぶには**最も重要な博物館です。

▶ 奈良国立博物館は午前9時半**から午後5時まで開いています**が、チケット売場は午後4時半**に閉まります**。

▶ 奈良国立博物館は、毎週月曜日と1月1日が**休館となります**。

▶ 奈良国立博物館は、毎週月曜日が休館で、月曜日が**祝日**の場合は翌日の火曜日が休館になります。

▶ 奈良国立博物館には、英語のガイド**があります**。

Facility

▶ The Nara National Museum is the most important museum **for learning about** ancient Japanese history.

▶ The Nara National Museum **is open between** 9:30 a.m. **and** 5:00 p.m., and the ticket window **closes at** 4:30 p.m.

▶ The Nara National Museum **is closed on** Mondays and January 1.

▶ The Nara National Museum is closed on Mondays, but if Monday is a **public holiday**, the museum will be closed on Tuesday.

▶ An English guide **is available** at the Nara National Museum.

3 道順

外国の人から道をきかれたときの対応例を集めました。ここにある基本的な単語や熟語を使えば、たいていの案内はこなせるはずです。

▶ 言問橋を東京スカイツリー**に向かって、歩いて渡って**ください。

▶ 銀座通り**に沿って歩いて**ください。新橋は交差点から 800 メートルほどです。

▶ 鳥居をくぐる**と**、神社の本殿が**見えてきます**。

▶ 鳥居をくぐったら最初の脇道を**右に曲がります**。すると日本の器を扱う専門店があります。

▶ 四条河原町の交差点を**左に曲がって**ください。

▶ 合羽橋の交差点**を右に曲がって**ください。

Route

▶ **Walk across** the Kototoi-bashi Bridge **toward** the Tokyo Sky Tree.

▶ **Walk along** Ginza-dori Street. Shinbashi is 800 meters from this intersection.

▶ **After** pass**ing** under this torii gate, **you can see** the main hall of this shrine.

▶ After passing under this torii gate, **turn to the right** on the first side street, and you will find a shop which specializes in Japanese pottery.

▶ **Turn left at** Shijo Kawaramachi intersection.

▶ **Turn right at** Kappabashi intersection.

▶ 三越デパート**まで戻りましょう。**

▶ 薬師寺を訪ねたら、**すぐとなりにある**唐招提寺というお寺**にも行きましょう。**

▶ この大きな交差点**を渡って**2番目の路地**を右に曲がって**ください。文膳というレストラン**があります。**

▶ 御堂筋**を南へ**500メートルほど、心斎橋の方**へ行って**ください。

▶ 橋の**すぐ手前を**右に曲がって、小さな路地を**歩いて**ください。すると狐**を奉った**可愛い神社があります。

▶ 銀座四丁目の交差点**に行く途中**、伊東屋という文房具屋を**見逃さないように。**

▶ 松坂屋は、あなたの**左手に**あります。

▶ **Let's go back to** Mitsukoshi Department Store.

▶ After visiting Yakushi-ji Temple, **you will see** another temple called Toshodai-ji, which **is located just next to** Yakushi-ji.

▶ **After crossing** this big intersection, **turn to the right at** the second alley. **You will find** a restaurant called Fumizen.

▶ **Go south on** Midosuji Street for about 500 meters to the Shinsaibashi area.

▶ Turn right **just before** the bridge and **walk into** the small alley. You will find a cute shrine **dedicated to** foxes.

▶ **On the way to** Ginza-yon-chome intersection, **don't miss** the stationery shop called Ito-ya.

▶ Matsuzakaya Department Store is located **on your left**.

▶ 明治通り**を行きましょう**。左側に伊勢丹があ
ります。

▶ JR 両国駅**を降りて目の前にある**建物が国技
館で、そこが相撲**の本拠地**です。

▶ 銀座四丁目の交差点を東銀座方向に**東に歩い
て**ください。昭和通り**を渡って**すぐ左側に歌
舞伎座が見えてきます。

▶ **Let's take** the street called Meiji-dori. Isetan Department Store is on your left.

▶ When you **come out of** JR Ryogoku Station, the building standing right **in front of** you is the Kokugikan, the **home of** Japanese sumo.

▶ **Walk east** from the Ginza-yon-chome intersection toward Higashi-ginza. **Cross** Showa-dori Street, and immediately to the left you will see the Kabuki-za Theater.

4 店舗

店舗の説明です。specialize in（〜を専門にしている）という表現は知っておくと大変便利です。また、「何々を扱っている」、あるいは「商っている」という言葉は sell のほかに carry、deal with、offer または簡単に have という言葉でも表現できます。

▶ この店は日本の器**の専門店**です。

▶ 備前屋というこの店は、日本の漬け物**の専門店**です。

▶ この店は日本の包丁**の専門店**です。

▶ 左側には日本舞踊で使う扇子**を売る**店があります。

▶ この店は日本の伝統的な扇子**を扱っています**。

▶ この地域には日常品**を扱う**店が集まっています。

Shop

▶ This shop **specializes in** Japanese pottery.

▶ This shop called Bizen-ya, **specializes in** Japanese pickles.

▶ This shop **specializes in** Japanese kitchen knives.

▶ On your left, there is a store **selling** fans for use in traditional Japanese dance.

▶ This shop **carries** *sensu*, or traditional Japanese folding fans.

▶ This area has shops **dealing with** everyday goods.

▶ 藤屋は日本の手ぬぐい**を専門に売る**店です。

▶ 鳩居堂では、伝統的な和紙**を売っ**ています。

▶ この店では美しい染めの着物**を売っ**ています。

▶ この店では伝統的な漆の家具**を扱っ**ています。漆の家具はとても高価です。

▶ この店では、小さくて手ごろな値段の物**のほかに**、とても高価な漆の器**も売っ**ています。

▶ Fuji-ya is a shop **specializing in** *tenugui*, or Japanese towels.

▶ The shop called Kyukyo-do **offers** traditional Japanese paper.

▶ This shop **has** beautifully dyed kimonos.

▶ This shop **carries** traditional Japanese lacquer furniture. It is very expensive.

▶ This shop **carries** very expensive lacquer bowls **as well as** other small, affordable items.

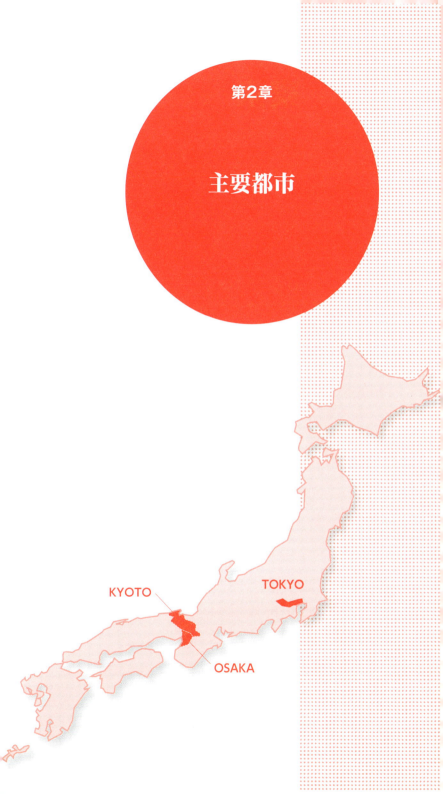

第2章

主要都市

KYOTO

TOKYO

OSAKA

1 東京

世界最大の都市の一つとして、東京都 23 区には 900 万人超の人が住み、東京が位置する関東平野の隣接する都市まで数えると、首都圏は世界で最も人口の多い大都市となり、その合わせた人口は 3500 万人を超えます。
東京の歴史、経済的な躍動感、文化遺産、素晴らしい料理などを英語で説明してみましょう。

▶ 東京は、日本の首都で、行政、立法、司法の中心地です。

▶ 東京は日本列島の中央にある、日本で最も大きな都市です。

▶ 東京には、1300 万人の人が住んでいます。

▶ 東京は 23 の区からなる、いわゆる特別区と、その他の市町村による地域からできています。

Tokyo

▶ Since Tokyo is the capital of Japan, it is the center of government, the legislature and the judiciary.

▶ Tokyo is located in the middle of the Japanese archipelago, and it is Japan's largest city.

▶ There are 13 million people living in Tokyo.

▶ Tokyo is made up of 23 so-called special wards plus a collection of sub-cities, towns and villages.

第2章

主要都市

29

▶ 太平洋にある伊豆諸島と小笠原諸島も東京都の一部となります。

▶ 東京都の都内総生産は約92兆9000億円です。

▶ 東京都の経済規模は、カリフォルニア州の約半分です。

▶ 東京は、アメリカのオクラホマシティ、イランのテヘランと同じ緯度に位置しています。

▶ 東京都の年間予算は約13兆円です。

▶ 山手線と呼ばれる東京の環状線沿いの駅には、商業、ビジネス、文化の中心が集まっています。

▶ 東京23区のうち、千代田区には国の行政機関や金融機関が集まっています。

▶ The Izu and Ogasawara archipelagos, which lie in the Pacific Ocean, are also part of Tokyo.

▶ Tokyo's GDP is around 92.9 trillion yen.

▶ Tokyo's economy is about half the size of California's economy.

▶ Tokyo is at the same latitude as Oklahoma City in the U.S. and Tehran in Iran.

▶ Tokyo's annual budget is around 13 trillion yen.

▶ The Yamanote line is a railway loop line in Tokyo, and several commercial, business and cultural hubs are located at stations along the line.

▶ One of Tokyo's 23 wards, Chiyoda Ward, is home to many of the country's government and financial institutions.

▶ 港区には、麻布や六本木といった国際色豊かな繁華街があり、東京を代表する商業の中心地です。

▶ 皇居の正門から広い道路を少し行くと東京駅があり、そこから地方へ無数の鉄道網が伸びています。

▶ 東京都庁は、新宿副都心という高層ビル街の一画を成しています。

▶ かつて江戸城であった皇居は、東京の中心にあります。

▶ 東京の西は、富士山などで有名な山岳地帯に面しています。

▶ 東京では、桜は4月初旬に一斉に開花します。

▶ Minato Ward, which includes the cosmopolitan commercial centers of Azabu and Roppongi, is one of Tokyo's business centers.

▶ A wide boulevard leads from the Imperial Palace to Tokyo Station, where numerous rail lines connect Tokyo to the provinces.

▶ Tokyo City Hall is part of the skyscraper district called Shinjuku Sub-Center.

▶ The Imperial Palace, which used to be Edo Castle, is located in the center of Tokyo.

▶ To the west, Tokyo faces several mountains, the most famous of which is Mt. Fuji.

▶ Cherry blossoms bloom in Tokyo at the beginning of April.

▶ 6月から7月にかけて、東京は梅雨という雨期になります。

▶ 東京の夏はとても蒸し暑いです。

▶ 東京に雪が降るのは一冬に多くても数回ですが、雪に慣れていないので、多くの都市機能に影響がでます。

▶ 渋滞を考えれば、東京での移動は鉄道や地下鉄がおすすめです。

▶ 東京駅から、新幹線が日本の主要都市に向けて出発します。

▶ 東京には羽田と成田の二つの国際空港があります。

▶ 羽田空港は東京にあり、国内線と国際線が発着しています。

▶ In June and July Tokyo has a rainy season, which is called *tsuyu*.

▶ Tokyo summers are hot and humid.

▶ Tokyo sees snow a few times at most each winter, and since Tokyo isn't accustomed to regular snowfall, many city functions can be disrupted when it snows.

▶ Considering the traffic, the best way to get around the city is by train or subway.

▶ From Tokyo Station, bullet trains depart for major cities across Japan.

▶ Tokyo has two international airports, Haneda and Narita.

▶ Haneda Airport is located in Tokyo and is served by domestic and international routes.

▶ 成田空港は、東京の北東約 80 キロの位置に
あります。

▶ 東京では、水道の水は飲んでも問題はありま
せん。

▶ 東京も含め、日本中どこでもチップの習慣は
ありません。

▶ 東京の都市部では、クレジットカードを使え
る場所が増えましたが、海外と比べるとまだ
現金社会です。

▶ 東京は比較的治安がいいので、多くの現金を
持ち歩いても大丈夫です。

▶ 東京では外食文化が発達してます。

▶ 東京の朝食文化はあまり発達していません

▶ ほとんどの飲食店はランチからの営業です。

▶ Narita Airport is located 80 kilometers to the northeast of Tokyo.

▶ It is safe to drink the tap water in Tokyo.

▶ In Tokyo, as well as in the rest of Japan, there is no custom of tipping.

▶ More and more places in Tokyo accept credit cards, but it's still a cash society compared to other countries.

▶ Because Tokyo is relatively safe, it is okay to carry a large amount of cash.

▶ Tokyo has a big culture of eating out.

▶ Tokyo doesn't have much of a breakfast culture.

▶ Most restaurants are only open from lunchtime.

▶ カラオケ店、漫画喫茶などは一晩中開いている店もあります。

▶ ディナーは高くても、ランチは手頃な価格で出しているというレストランがたくさんあります。

▶ ランチセットの定番を定食といい、メインディッシュ1皿に、ご飯、味噌汁、漬物という献立です。

▶ ビックカメラや山田電気、ヨドバシカメラといった「欲しいものはなんでもある」家電量販店では、海外では見られないようなユニークな家電やその付属品を見つけることができます。

▶ 浅草の合羽橋通り界隈には、家庭の台所やレストランで使用する料理用具を売る店が並んでいます。

▶ Some of Karaoke parlors and manga cafés stay open all night.

▶ Many restaurants that are quite expensive for dinner offer reasonably priced lunches.

▶ A typical lunch set is called a *teishoku*, and includes one main dish along with rice, miso soup and pickles.

▶ We think you will encounter truly unique household electrical goods and accessories, of the sort you will not find anywhere overseas, at well-stocked electric-goods shops such as Bic Camera, Yamada Electrical and Yodobashi Camera.

▶ In the Kappabashi-dori neighborhood near Asakusa, the streets are lined with shops selling cooking utensils for both restaurants and home kitchens.

▶ デパ地下では、日本をはじめ世界中のさまざまな食料品や酒類を購入できます。さらに、伝統的な和菓子や洋菓子も揃っています。

▶ 皇居は日本の天皇家の住む所です。

▶ 皇居は東京の真ん中にあります。

▶ 皇居は千代田区にあり、近くには東京駅があります。

▶ 皇居の下は地下鉄が通っていません。

▶ 皇居の敷地面積は、ニューヨークにあるセントラルパークのおよそ３倍です。

▶ 銀座は東京でも最も高価なレストランやバーのある街です。

▶ *Depa-chika* are places where you can purchase a wide variety of food and alcohol from Japan and around the world, including traditional Japanese and Western-style sweets.

▶ The Imperial Palace is the home of Japan's Imperial family.

▶ The Imperial Palace is located in the center of Tokyo.

▶ The Imperial Palace is located near Tokyo Station, in Chiyoda Ward.

▶ No subway lines pass under the Imperial Palace.

▶ The Imperial Palace grounds are about three times the size of New York City's Central Park.

▶ Ginza has some of the most expensive restaurants and bars in the city.

▶ 銀座には、一人前で数百ドルもする寿司屋が
あります。

▶ 中央通りは、銀座のメインストリートです。

▶ 週末の午後、中央通りは車の通行を禁じ、歩
行者天国になります。

▶ 浅草には、東京で最も有名な浅草寺という寺
があります。

▶ 浅草では昔ながらの人力車に乗ることができ
ます。

▶ 浅草は昔から職人たちが住む地区です。

▶ 浅草には、伝統工芸品を売る店があります。

▶ In Ginza, a sushi dinner for one person can cost several hundred dollars.

▶ Chuo Street is the main street in Ginza.

▶ Chuo Street is closed to cars on weekend afternoons, turning it into a so-called "pedestrian heaven."

▶ Asakusa is the home of Senso-ji, Tokyo's most famous temple.

▶ You can ride in a traditional rickshaw in Asakusa.

▶ Asakusa was traditionally a neighborhood where craftsmen lived.

▶ In Asakusa you can find stores selling traditional crafts.

▶ 浅草には江戸時代から営業を続ける料理屋が
あります。

▶ 東京には、いくつかの外国人コミュニティが
あります。新大久保には韓国人、江戸川区に
はインド人、高田馬場にはミャンマー人、東
京都に隣接する埼玉県蕨市にはクルド人など
が集まっています。

▶ 東京都とその周辺には6万人以上の留学生が
生活しています。

▶ There are restaurants in Asakusa that have been in business since the Edo era.

▶ There are several foreign communities in Tokyo, including the Korean community in Shin-Okubo, the Indian community in Edogawa Ward, the Myanmar community in Takadanobaba, and the Kurdish community in Warabi City in neighboring Saitama Prefecture.

▶ There are more than 60,000 foreign exchange students in and around Tokyo.

2 大阪

日本の文化の中心、京都にほど近く、また西日本最大の都市として発展したため、独自の文化を築いてきた大阪。そこは、全国からあらゆる食材が集まる「天下の台所」であり、瀬戸内の海産物や大阪近郊の野菜にも恵まれ、日本料理の基礎となった食文化が栄え、「大阪の食い倒れ」という諺まで生まれました。

また、商業の町として角の立たない円滑な話術が発達し、上方落語、漫才、吉本新喜劇・松竹新喜劇などのお笑い文化が栄えています。

▶ 大阪は東京から 550 キロ西のところに位置しています。

▶ 東京と大阪の間は、新幹線で 2 時間半かかります。

▶ 大阪は、日本で 2 番目に大きな商業の中心地です。

▶ もともとの大阪城は、豊臣秀頼が徳川家康に滅ぼされた 1615 年に壊されました。

Osaka

▶ Osaka is a city located about 550 kilometers west of Tokyo.

▶ It takes two hours and thirty minutes to travel between Tokyo and Osaka by Shinkansen.

▶ Osaka is the second-largest commercial center in Japan.

▶ The original Osaka Castle was destroyed when Toyotomi Hideyori was defeated by Tokugawa Ieyasu in 1615.

▶ 徳川家康は 1603 年、江戸（現東京）に幕府を開き、12 年後に大阪城の豊臣秀頼を倒しました。

▶ 江戸時代、文楽が大阪で始まりました。

▶ 大阪は商人魂で有名です。大阪の商人を「大阪商人」と呼びます。

▶ 阪神タイガースは大阪地区をベースにする人気のプロ野球チームで、東京をベースにする読売ジャイアンツとはライバル同士です。

▶ 大阪駅のある梅田は、大阪のビジネスの中心です。

▶ 難波は大阪の商業の中心で、梅田の南側に位置してます。

▶ Tokugawa Ieyasu founded the shogunate in Edo, which is now called Tokyo, in 1603 and defeated Toyotomi Hideyori at Osaka Castle 12 years later.

▶ In the Edo period, *bunraku* puppet theater was created in Osaka.

▶ Osaka is famous for its merchant spirit. Osaka's merchants are called *Osaka-shonin.*

▶ The Hanshin Tigers are a very popular professional baseball team based in the Osaka area and are the rivals of the Yomiuri Giants, who are based in Tokyo.

▶ Umeda, where Osaka Station is located, is Osaka's business center.

▶ Nanba is Osaka's commercial center and is located south of Umeda.

▶ 大阪の鉄道の玄関は新大阪で、大阪駅の北東
　５キロのところにあります。

▶ 大阪の国際空港は街の南側にあり、関西国際
　空港といいます。

▶ 大阪の国内線向け空港は、大阪国際空港（伊
　丹空港）といいます。

▶ 西から東へ、神戸、大阪、京都の３都市は、
　大阪都市圏を形成しています。

▶ 大阪を中心とした広域圏を関西といいます。

▶ Osaka's rail gateway is Shin-Osaka, located five kilometers northeast of Osaka Station.

▶ Osaka's international airport is located south of the city and is named Kansai International Airport.

▶ Osaka's domestic airport is called Osaka International Airport, or Itami Airport.

▶ From west to east, Kobe, Osaka, and Kyoto are the three major cities making up the Greater Osaka Area.

▶ The Greater Osaka Area is called Kansai in Japanese.

3 京都

明治天皇が東京に行幸するまでの約 1080 年にわたって天皇家および公家が集住したため、京都は「千年の都」との雅称で呼ばれています。
第二次世界大戦の戦災被害を免れた神社仏閣、古い史跡、町並みが数多く存在し、宗教・貴族・武家・庶民などの様々な歴史的文化や祭りが国内外の観光客を引き寄せる世界有数の観光都市です。さらに、京都大学をはじめとする多数の大学が集積し、国内外から学生や研究者が集まる学園都市ともなっています。

▷ 京都は 794 年から 1869 年の間、日本の首都でした。

▷ 京都は盆地に位置してます。

▷ 京都は東京の西、460 キロのところに位置してます。

▷ 東京から京都までは、新幹線で 2 時間 15 分かかります。

▷ 大阪から京都までは、電車で 30 分ほどです。

Kyoto

▶ Kyoto was the capital of Japan between 794 and 1869.

▶ Kyoto is located in a basin.

▶ Kyoto is located about 460 kilometers west of Tokyo.

▶ It takes two hours and fifteen minutes from Tokyo to Kyoto by Shinkansen.

▶ It takes only 30 minutes from Osaka to Kyoto by commuter train.

▶ 京都は古都ということだけでなく、日本の文化の中心です。

▶ 忙しい現代社会に暮らす日本の人たちにしてみると、京都は精神的な癒しの場でもあります。

▶ 美しい庭のある古い寺、神社、別荘、伝統の家など、数えきれない名所旧跡が京都にはあります。

▶ 2006 年には、4800 万人以上の人が京都を訪れています。

▶ 京都の名所旧跡や遺産には、毎年 80 万人の海外の人が訪れています。

▶ 京都には 3000 以上の寺や神社があります。

▶ 京都にある多くの建築物や庭は、国宝です。

▶ Kyoto is not only the old capital but also the country's cultural heart.

▶ Kyoto is a place for spiritual healing among Japanese people living in a busy, modern society.

▶ In Kyoto, you can enjoy countless historical sites, such as old temples with beautiful gardens, shrines, villas, and traditional houses.

▶ More than 48 million visitors came to Kyoto in 2006.

▶ About 800,000 visitors from abroad enjoy Kyoto's historical sites and heritage every year.

▶ There are more than 3,000 temples and shrines in Kyoto.

▶ Many of the buildings and gardens in Kyoto are national treasures.

▶ 京都には、様々な仏教宗派の本部になっている寺が、数多くあります。

▶ 天皇が宮廷を京都に移すことにしたのは、794年のことでした。

▶ 1192年以降、将軍が鎌倉で政治を行うようになってからも、天皇は京都の朝廷にとどまっていました。

▶ 15世紀、京都は10年におよぶ応仁の乱で焼け野原になりました。

▶ 1603年に徳川家康は将軍に任命され、江戸（現東京）に幕府を開きましたが、天皇は京都に残りました。

▶ 今でも、京都御所と呼ばれる宮廷が京都にはあります。

▶ In Kyoto, there are many temples that serve as the headquarters of various Buddhist sects.

▶ It was in 794 that the emperor decided to move his court to Kyoto.

▶ Even after 1192, when a general called a shogun started his own government in Kamakura, the emperor remained at Kyoto's imperial court.

▶ In the fifteenth century, Kyoto was burned during a 10-year period of battles called the Onin War.

▶ In 1603, when Tokugawa Ieyasu was appointed shogun, he founded his government in Edo, which is now called Tokyo, while the emperor's court remained in Kyoto.

▶ Even now, there remains a palace in Kyoto called Kyoto Gosho.

▶ 天皇家は、重要な儀式があるときはいつでも京都御所を訪れます。

▶ 古い商家を町家といい、京都のあちこちにあります。

▶ 京都の繁華街は河原町で、鴨川の西岸に位置しています。

▶ 鴨川の西側には先斗町があり、古くからの料理屋が立ち並んでいます。

▶ 祇園は国の歴史保存地区で、古くからの民家、お茶屋、料理屋などがあります。

▶ 京都では芸者のことを芸妓と呼びます。彼女たちは、伝統的なお茶屋や料理屋で働くプロの芸人です。

▶ The emperor's family visits Kyoto Gosho whenever an important celebration takes place.

▶ *Machiya* is the name given to old merchant houses, and you can find many of them in Kyoto.

▶ Kyoto's commercial center is Kawaramachi, which is located along the west bank of the Kamo River.

▶ On the western side of the Kamo River, you will find the Pontocho district, which is lined with traditional restaurants.

▶ Gion is a national historic preservation district where you will see many old houses, tea houses called *ochaya*, and restaurants.

▶ In Kyoto, geisha are called *geiko*. They are professional entertainers at traditional tea houses and restaurants.

▶ 舞妓はまだ修行中の芸妓のことで、祇園あたりでは着物を着て、髪を結った舞妓たちを見かけます。

▶ 芸妓は遊女ではありません。芸妓とは洗練された身のこなしで、パトロンや大切な顧客を楽しませる女性のことです。

▶ 清水寺から銀閣寺まで、東山地区には多くの名だたる寺があります。

▶ 金閣寺、妙心寺、そして龍安寺は、北山地区にあります。

▶ いくつかの歴史的な家屋や寺を訪ねるには、予約が必要です。

▶ A *maiko* is a *geiko* in training, and you will see them in their traditional kimonos and hair styles in the Gion area.

▶ *Geiko* are not prostitutes. A *geiko* is a lady with elegant manners who entertains patrons and important customers.

▶ Between Kiyomizu-dera Temple and Ginkaku-ji Temple, there are many famous temples in the mountainous Higashiyama area.

▶ Kinkaku-ji, Myoshin-ji, and Ryoan-ji temples are located in the Kitayama area.

▶ You need to make a reservation to visit some historical villas and temples.

第3章

北海道

HOKKAIDO

1 基本情報

▶ 北海道は最も北にある島で、冬の寒さはとても厳しいです。

▶ 北海道は日本の4つの主な島のうちのひとつで、本州のすぐ北に位置しています。

▶ 北海道は日本で2番目に大きい島ですが、人口は550万人ほどです。

2 交通

▶ 東京から北海道へ行くには、青函トンネルを通って津軽海峡を渡る夜行列車がおすすめです。

▶ 新千歳空港は、北海道の空の玄関です。

Basic Tips

▶ Hokkaido is the northernmost island, and it can be bitterly cold in winter.

▶ Hokkaido is one of the four major islands of Japan, and it is located just north of Honshu.

▶ Hokkaido is the second-largest island in Japan, with only 5.5 million people.

Transportation

▶ To access Hokkaido from Tokyo, it is a good idea to take the night train running through the Seikan Tunnel under the Tsugaru Strait.

▶ New Chitose Airport is the air gateway to Hokkaido.

3 気候と地勢

▶ 北海道の冬はとても寒く、スキーリゾートも
たくさんあります。

▶ 北海道の東側の沿岸には大量の流氷が流れ着
き、見事です。

▶ 北海道は、日本の他の地域のように混んでい
ません。実際、広大な空地がたくさんありま
す。

4 主要都市

▶ 札幌は北海道の道庁所在地であり、商業の中
心です。

▶ 札幌では2月初旬に雪祭りが行われ、野外に
ディスプレイされた雪の像などを楽しめま
す。

Climate and Geographical Feature

▶ In winter, it is very cold in Hokkaido, and you will find many ski resorts there.

▶ You can see huge amounts of beautiful drift ice reach the eastern seashore of Hokkaido.

▶ Hokkaido is not crowded like other parts of Japan. In fact, it has many wide open spaces.

Main Cities

▶ Sapporo is the capital and commercial center of Hokkaido.

▶ There is a snow festival in early February in Sapporo where you can enjoy many snow sculptures displayed outdoors.

▶ 函館は昔からの港町で、北海道の海からの玄関口となっています。

5 北方領土

▶ 千島列島（クリル諸島）は、北東沿岸に位置しています。

▶ クリル諸島の4島について、日本とロシア双方が領土だと主張し合っています。

6 アイヌ

▶ 北海道にはアイヌという民族が住んでいます。

▶ アイヌは北海道の先住民族で、日本の他の地域とは異なるユニークな文化を持っています。

▶ Hakodate is an old port town and the ocean gateway to Hokkaido.

The Northern Territories

▶ The Chishima-retto, or Kuril Islands, is located off the northeastern coast.

▶ There is a territorial dispute between Japan and Russia over four of the Kuril Islands.

Ainu

▶ Hokkaido is where the ethnic group called the *Ainu* live.

▶ The *Ainu* are an indigenous tribe living in Hokkaido, and they have a unique culture that is very different from that of the rest of Japan.

7 歴史的背景

▶ 北海道の大部分は 19 世紀に拓かれました。

▶ 19 世紀の北海道は開拓地でした。そのため、歴史的背景や雰囲気がまったく他の日本の地域とは違っています。

▶ 北海道への定住が始まったのは 19 世紀ごろで、日本の他の地域と比べると、非常に遅れていました。

Historical Background

▶ Many parts of Hokkaido were settled around the nineteenth century.

▶ Hokkaido was Japan's frontier in the nineteenth century. Therefore, the atmosphere and historical background are quite different from other parts of Japan.

▶ Many parts of Hokkaido were settled around the nineteenth century, much later than other parts of Japan.

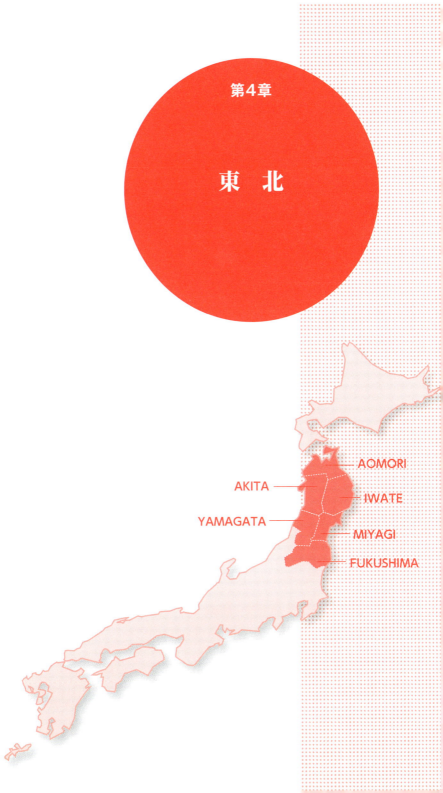

第4章

東　北

AOMORI
AKITA
IWATE
YAMAGATA
MIYAGI
FUKUSHIMA

1 基本情報

▶ 東北は本州北部のことで、北海道とは津軽海峡で隔てられています。

▶ 東北には6つの県があります。

▶ 秋田と山形は、日本海に面しています。

▶ 岩手、宮城、そして福島は太平洋に面しています。

2 交通

▶ 東北と北海道は、青函トンネルという鉄道トンネルで結ばれています。

▶ 東京から東北に行くには、新幹線を利用するのが便利です。

Basic Tips

▶ Tohoku makes up the northern part of Honshu and is separated from Hokkaido by a channel called the Tsugaru Strait.

▶ There are six prefectures in Tohoku.

▶ Akita and Yamagata prefectures face the Sea of Japan.

▶ Iwate, Miyagi, and Fukushima prefectures face the Pacific Ocean.

Transportation

▶ Tohoku and Hokkaido are connected by a train tunnel called the Seikan Tunnel.

▶ It is convenient to use the Shinkansen to visit Tohoku from Tokyo.

3 自然

▶ 東北は山、湖、そして複雑に海岸線が入り組んでいることで知られる三陸海岸などが有名です。

▶ 三陸海岸は東北の太平洋側で、その美しい海岸線で知られています。

4 伝統・文化

▶ 東北は夏祭りでよく知られています。

▶ 仙台は七夕祭りで有名です。七夕祭りは星座の伝説に基づいています。

▶ 青森県のねぶた祭は、豪華な装飾が施された山車がよく知られています。

Nature

▶ Tohoku is famous for its mountains, lakes, and complexly etched coastline known as the Sanriku Kaigan.

▶ The Sanriku Kaigan is located on the Pacific side of Tohoku and is known for its beautiful coastline.

Tradition and Culture

▶ Tohoku is famous for its summer festivals.

▶ Sendai is famous for its Tanabata Festival. The Tanabata Festival is based on a Zodiac legend.

▶ The Nebuta Festival in Aomori Prefecture is famous for its beautifully decorated floats.

▶ 夏に秋田で行われる竿燈祭りでは、伝統的な日本の提灯を付けた大きな飾りを持って人々が練り歩きます。

▶ 東北は民芸品で有名です。

▶ 東北のこけしは、昔からの木製の人形で、主に山形で作られています。

▶ 座敷童は、子供の幽霊のことです。座敷童は古い家々を害から守ると東北では言われています。

▶ なまはげは、秋田地方の鬼のことです。冬の祭りのとき、なまはげは家々を訪れ、親の言うことを聞くようにと子供たちを怖がらせます。

▶ The Kanto Festival is held in Akita City in summer, and people march with towers of traditional Japanese lanterns.

▶ Tohoku is famous for its local folk art.

▶ *Kokeshi* traditional wooden dolls from Tohoku and are mainly produced in Yamagata.

▶ *Zashiki-warashi* is the name given to the ghosts of children. It is said that they keep the old houses in Tohoku safe from harm.

▶ *Namahage* is the name given to ogres in the Akita area. During a winter festival, they visit each household to threaten children into listening to their parents.

5 青森県

▶ 東北の最北の県は青森です。

▶ 津軽は青森県の西で、リンゴで有名です。

▶ 十和田湖は青森県にあり、湖周辺は美しい
山々、川、温泉などがあります。

Aomori

▶ The northernmost prefecture in Tohoku is Aomori.

▶ Tsugaru is the western area of Aomori Prefecture and is famous for its apples.

▶ Lake Towada-ko is located in Aomori Prefecture, and around the lake are beautiful mountains, streams, and hot springs.

第4章

東北

6 秋田県

▶ 秋田県は，東北の北西にあり、冬期の豪雪で知られています。

▶ 田沢湖は秋田県の行楽地です。

▶ 秋田県に行ったら、角館を訪ねてください。封建時代からの武家屋敷がよく保存されています。

Akita

▶ Akita Prefecture is located in the northwest part of Tohoku and is known for its heavy snowfalls in winter.

▶ Lake Tazawa-ko is a resort area in Akita Prefecture.

▶ When you visit Akita Prefecture, do not forget to visit Kakunodate, a well-preserved samurai town from the feudal period.

第4章

東北

7 岩手県

▶ 盛岡は岩手県の県庁所在地で、かつては南部氏の所領でした。城跡は今でも街の中心に残っています。

▶ 岩手の太平洋側は三陸といい、風光明媚なリアス式海岸でよく知られています。

▶ 遠野は岩手にある村ですが、民間伝承で有名な町です。

▶ 平泉は歴史のある町で、12 世紀に権勢を振るった藤原氏の本拠地だったところです。

▶ 岩手県の太平洋岸は、東日本大震災の津波で壊滅的な被害を受けました。

Iwate

▶ Morioka is the capital of Iwate Prefecture and was once the home of the Nanbu clan. The ruins of their castle are still in the center of the city.

▶ The Pacific Ocean side of Iwate is called Sanriku and is known for its picturesque sawtooth coastline.

▶ Tono is a village in Iwate and is famous for its folk heritage.

▶ Hiraizumi is a historic town where the once-powerful Fujiwara clan constructed their headquarters in the twelfth century.

▶ The Pacific coast of Iwate Prefecture suffered terrible destruction in the tsunami after the 2011 Tohoku Earthquake.

8 宮城県

▶ 宮城県には仙台市があります。仙台は東北地
方の中心です。

▶ 仙台の青葉城は、封建時代に最も勢力の大き
かった家の一つ伊達家の居城でした。

▶ 松島は宮城県の北部にある美しい海辺のこと
です。

Miyagi

▶ Miyagi is the prefecture where the city of Sendai is located. Sendai is the regional capital of Tohoku.

▶ Aoba Castle in Sendai was the home of the Date clan, one of the most powerful families during the feudal period.

▶ Matsushima is a beautiful coastal area located in the northern part of Miyagi Prefecture.

9 山形県

▶ 山形県は秋田の南に位置し、日本海に面しています。

▶ 蔵王は山形県にある山で、スキーリゾートとして知られています。

▶ 出羽三山は山形県にある3つの山で、古代より霊山として知られています。

Yamagata

▶ Yamagata Prefecture is located south of Akita and faces the Sea of Japan.

▶ Zao is a mountain in Yamagata Prefecture and is known for its ski resort.

▶ Dewa Sanzan are three mountains located in Yamagata Prefecture, and they have been known as spiritual places since ancient times.

10 福島県

▶ 福島県は東北南部に位置し、県庁所在地は福島市です。

▶ 会津若松はお城で有名です。

▶ 東北の南部にある会津地方では、美しい湖や山が楽しめます。

▶ 会津地方は、1868年に徳川幕府終焉の際、激しい戦いが行われた場所です。

▶ 福島県は、東日本大震災の津波による、福島第一原子力発電所のメルトダウンで大変苦しんでいます。

Fukushima

▶ Fukushima Prefecture lies in the southern part of Tohoku, and its capital is Fukushima City.

▶ Aizu Wakamatsu is famous for its castle.

▶ Aizu is in the southern part of Tohoku, where you can enjoy beautiful lakes and mountains.

▶ Aizu was the site of a terrible battle when the Tokugawa Shogunate came to an end in 1868.

▶ Fukushima Prefecture was seriously affected by the nuclear meltdown of Fukushima Dai Ichi Nuclear Power Plant due to the tsunami after the 2011 Tohoku Earthquake.

第4章

東北

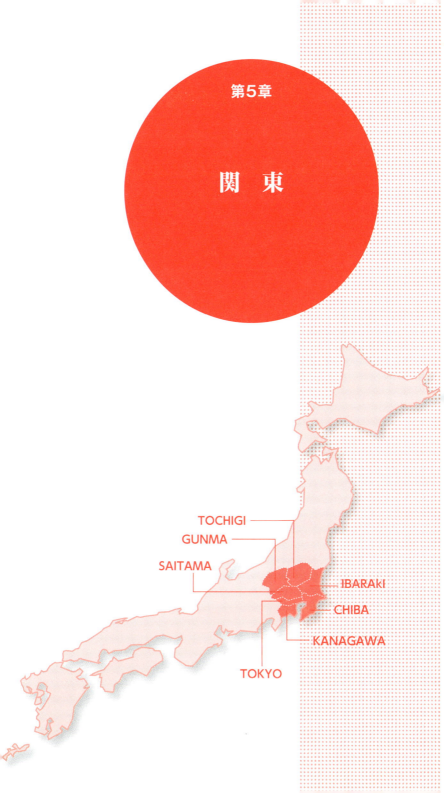

第5章

関東

TOCHIGI
GUNMA
SAITAMA
IBARAKI
CHIBA
KANAGAWA
TOKYO

▶ 関東は本州の東部中央に位置し、日本の中心です。

▶ 関東地方に、東京があります。

▶ 関東地方は東京都のほかに6県あります。

▶ 横浜は東京の南に位置する大都市で、江戸時代の終わりごろには外国人の居住区でした。

▶ 関東北部の群馬県と栃木県の山沿いは、興味深い温泉街がたくさんあります。

Basic Tips

▶ The east-central region of Japan called Kanto is the heart of the country.

▶ Kanto is the region of Japan where Tokyo is located.

▶ There are six prefectures in Kanto besides the Tokyo Metropolitan District.

▶ Yokohama is also a big city located south of Tokyo, where foreigners were allowed to live at the end of the Edo period.

▶ Around the mountainsides of Gunma and Tochigi prefectures, located in the northern area of Kanto, there are many interesting hot-spring villages.

2 地勢

▶ 関東の南部から中央にかけて、関東平野が広がっています。

▶ 関東北部から西部にかけては、山や温泉で有名です。

▶ 伊豆諸島は、太平洋側にある伊豆半島から南に連なっています。

3 交通

▶ 東京周辺には2つの国際空港があります。一つが成田空港で、もう一つが東京の中心からすぐの海沿いにある羽田空港です。

▶ 千葉県の成田空港は東京の中心部から列車で1時間ほどのところにあります。

Geographical Feature

▶ The central and southern parts of Kanto are on the Kanto Heiya, or Kanto Plain.

▶ The northern and western parts of Kanto are popular because of their mountains and hot springs.

▶ The Izu Islands stretch south from the Izu Peninsula in the Pacific Ocean.

Transportation

▶ There are two major international airports around Tokyo. One is Narita Airport, and the other is Haneda Airport, located near the ocean in central Tokyo.

▶ Narita Airport is in Chiba Prefecture and is located about a one-hour train ride from the center of Tokyo.

▶ 羽田国際空港は、国内線を利用するのにとても便利です。

▶ 羽田からは国際線も発着しています。

観光

▶ 成田で時間があれば、ぜひ成田市の新勝寺を訪ねてみてください。

▶ 東京からわずか2時間ほどのところにある日光は、日光東照宮という豪華な装飾の施された神社があり、人々に愛されています。

▶ 1192年から1333年の間、将軍がいた鎌倉には古寺や神社がたくさんあり、興味深い場所です。

▶ Haneda International Airport is quite convenient for domestic flights.

▶ International flights are also available from Haneda.

Sightseeing

▶ If you have time at Narita, it is a good idea to visit Shinsho-ji Temple in Narita City.

▶ Located just two hours from Tokyo, Nikko is loved for its magnificently decorated shrine called Nikko Tosho-gu.

▶ Kamakura, the seat of the shogunate between 1192 and 1333, is also an interesting place to visit because of its many old temples and shrines.

5 東京都

▶ 東京は東京都と呼ばれる特別行政区で、都内だけでなく、奥多摩など西部の山あいの地域も含まれています。

▶ 太平洋に浮かぶ伊豆と小笠原諸島は、東京都に属し、都内から 1000km にわたって点在しています。

▶ 日中、東京を歩き回るには公共交通がはるかに便利です。安い、早い、そして安全です。

Tokyo

▶ Tokyo is a special district called Tokyo-to, and it covers not only the city of Tokyo but the mountainous area called Okutama located west of the metropolis.

▶ Izu and the Ogasawara islands in the Pacific Ocean are part of Tokyo-to, and they stretch more than a thousand kilometers from the Tokyo metropolitan area.

▶ During the daytime, public transportation is by far the best way to get around central Tokyo; it's cheap, fast and very safe.

第5章

関東

6 群馬県

▶ 群馬県は関東の北西に位置し、前橋が県庁所在地です。

▶ 群馬には、草津、伊香保、水上など多くの有名な温泉があります。

▶ 群馬は昔、上州と呼ばれ、この地方の特長として乾燥した冬の風と、女性が強いことで知られています。

Gunma

▶ Gunma Prefecture is located in the northwest part of Kanto, and Maebashi is its capital.

▶ There are many famous hot springs in Gunma, such as Kusatsu, Ikaho, and Minakami.

▶ Gunma was once called Joshu, and this region was known for its dry winter wind and tough women.

第5章

関東

7 栃木県

▶ 栃木県は関東の中北部に位置し、県庁所在地は宇都宮市です。

▶ 栃木の山沿い地方を日光・那須といい、日本でも最も人気のある観光地の2つです。

▶ 面白いことに、栃木では餃子がよく食べられています。

Tochigi

▶ Tochigi Prefecture is in the north-central part of Kanto, and the prefectural capital is Utsunomiya City.

▶ The mountainous areas of Tochigi called Nikko and Nasu are two of the most popular tourist destinations in Japan.

▶ Interestingly, *gyoza*, or pot stickers, are Tochigi's main food product.

8 茨城県

▶ 茨城県は太平洋に面しており、県庁所在地の水戸は、偕楽園という伝統的な庭があることでよく知られています。

▶ 筑波研究学園都市には数多くの研究施設が集まっています。

▶ 茨城県の霞ヶ浦地方には多くの湖があります。

Ibaraki

▶ Ibaraki Prefecture faces the Pacific Ocean, and its prefectural capital, Mito, is known for its traditional garden called Kairaku-en.

▶ There are many research laboratories in Tsukuba Science City.

▶ Kasumigaura is an area of Ibaraki Prefecture where there are many lakes.

第5章

関東

9 埼玉県

▶ 埼玉県は東京の北に位置し、首都圏に属してます。

▶ 秩父と長瀞は、東京に住む人々にとってちょうどいい山あいのハイキングコースです。

▶ 埼玉の県庁所在地はさいたま市で、大宮が最大の都市です。

Saitama

▶ Saitama Prefecture is located north of Tokyo, and it is part of the Greater Tokyo Area.

▶ Chichibu and Nagatoro have good mountain hiking for the people of Tokyo.

▶ The capital of Saitama Prefecture is Saitama-city, and Omiya is the biggest city in that area.

第5章

関東

10 千葉県

▶ 千葉県は東京の東に位置し、東京のベッドタウンになっています。

▶ 千葉県の房総半島には、東京から多くの人がマリンスポーツを楽しみにやってきます。

▶ 成田国際空港は千葉県にあり、東京から電車で約1時間ほどです。

Chiba

▶ Chiba Prefecture is located east of Tokyo, and many parts of it are bedroom communities of Tokyo.

▶ Many people in Tokyo enjoy marine sports on the Boso Peninsula, located in Chiba Prefecture.

▶ Narita International Airport is located in Chiba Prefecture, and it takes approximately one hour to get there from Tokyo by train.

11 神奈川県

▶ 神奈川県は東京に隣接し、東京湾に面しています。

▶ 横浜は神奈川県の県庁所在地で、（東京から）電車で30分ほどです。

▶ 神奈川県の横浜、鎌倉は、史跡なども多いところです。

▶ 神奈川県は首都圏の人たちがマリンスポーツを楽しむ場所として人気があります。

▶ 箱根は、東京の近くにあって自然を満喫できる山間のリゾートです。

Kanagawa

▶ Kanagawa Prefecture is next door to Tokyo, facing Tokyo Bay.

▶ Yokohama is the capital of Kanagawa Prefecture, and it takes 30 minutes to get there by train.

▶ Kanagawa Prefecture's Yokohama and Kamakura have many historic sites.

▶ Kanagawa Prefecture is also a popular place for the people of the Tokyo Metropolitan Area to enjoy marine sports.

▶ Hakone is a mountainous resort area where you can enjoy natural beauty near Tokyo.

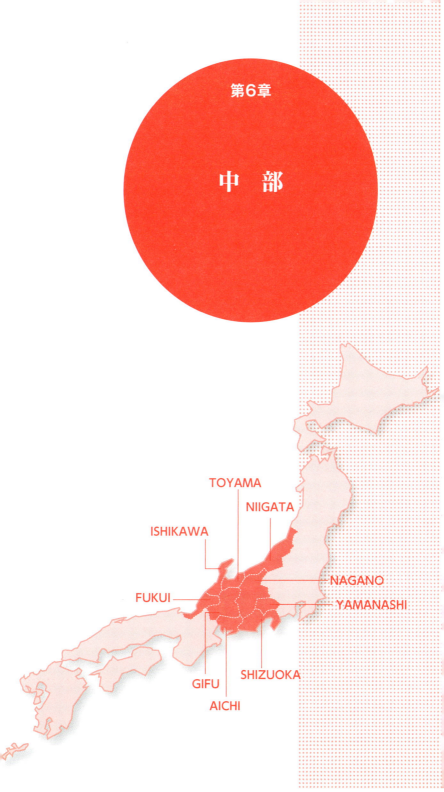

第6章

中　部

TOYAMA

NIIGATA

ISHIKAWA

NAGANO

YAMANASHI

FUKUI

GIFU

SHIZUOKA

AICHI

1 基本情報

▷ 中部地方は本州中部に位置する広大な地域の
ことです。

▷ 中部地方は日本海にも太平洋にも面していま
す。

▷ 中部地方には9つの県があり、最大の都市は
名古屋です。

▷ 名古屋およびその周辺は、日本で3番目に大
きな経済産業圏を形成しています。

▷ 中部国際空港は、海外から名古屋への空の玄
関です。

▷ 北陸地方の中心は金沢です。

Basic Tips

▶ The Chubu Region is a large area in the center of Honshu.

▶ The Chubu Region faces both the Sea of Japan and the Pacific Ocean.

▶ There are nine prefectures in the Chubu Region, and the biggest city in the area is Nagoya.

▶ Nagoya and its vicinity make up the third-largest industrial and economic zone in Japan.

▶ Chubu International Airport is the air gateway to Nagoya from abroad.

▶ Kanazawa is the regional center of the Hokuriku Region.

第6章

中部

2 自然

▶ 富士山は静岡県と山梨県の境にあり、その美しい姿で知られています。

▶ 富士山は美しく雄大な火山として日本の象徴になっています。

▶ 富士山は休火山で、標高 3776m と日本一の高さです。

▶ 中部地方には、日本アルプスという高い山脈がそびえています。

3 交通

▶ 中部地方の太平洋側にある主要都市は、東海道新幹線で結ばれています。

Nature

▶ Mt. Fuji is on the border between Shizuoka and Yamanashi prefectures, and it is well known for its beautiful shape.

▶ Mt. Fuji symbolizes Japan with its beautiful and majestic volcano shape.

▶ Mt. Fuji is a dormant volcano and the highest mountain in Japan at 3,776 meters.

▶ In the Chubu Region, there is a high mountain range called the Japan Alps.

第6章
中部

Transportation

▶ The major cities of the Pacific side of the Chubu Region are connected by the Tokaido Shinkansen.

▶ 東京と北陸地方は北陸新幹線で結ばれています。

▶ 日本アルプス方面に行くには、山沿いを通り東京と名古屋を結ぶ中央線を使うのが便利です。

▶ 小松空港は、福井県と石川県の2県で使用されています。

▶ The Hokuriku Region is connected with Tokyo by the Hokuriku Shinkansen.

▶ To reach the Japan Alps, it is convenient to take the Chuo Line connecting Tokyo and Nagoya via this mountainous area.

▶ Komatsu Airport serves both Fukui and Ishikawa prefectures.

4 北陸

▶ 中部地方のうち北部を北陸地方といいます。

▶ 中部地方の北部に位置し、日本海に面した北陸地方は、豪雪地帯として知られています。

▶ 北陸地方は積雪の多さで知られていましたが、最近は温暖化の影響で、それほどでもありません。

Hokuriku

▶ The Hokuriku area is in the northern part of the Chubu Region.

▶ The Hokuriku area, in the northern part of the Chubu Region and facing the Sea of Japan, is known for its heavy winter snowfalls.

▶ The Hokuriku Region was once known for its snow accumulations, but this has changed in recent years due to warmer weather.

第6章

中部

5 静岡県

▶ 静岡県は太平洋に面して広がっています。

▶ 伊豆半島は富士山と箱根に近く、国立公園の一部でもあります。

▶ 伊豆は比較的東京にも近く、温泉リゾートも数多くあります。

Shizuoka

▶ Shizuoka is a prefecture stretching along the Pacific Ocean.

▶ The Izu Peninsula is close to Mt. Fuji and Hakone, and is a part of a national park.

▶ Izu is relatively close to Tokyo and has many nice hot-spring resorts.

第6章

中部

6 山梨県

▶ 山梨県は静岡県の北に位置しています。

▶ 甲府盆地は、高い山に囲まれ、山梨県の真ん中に位置しています。

▶ 甲府は山梨県の県庁所在地で、その周辺はブドウ畑があることで知られています。

▶ 富士五湖は、富士山の麓にある山と湖の観光地です。

Yamanashi

▶ Yamanashi Prefecture is located north of Shizuoka.

▶ The Kofu Basin is surrounded by high mountains and is located in the center of Yamanashi Prefecture.

▶ Kofu is the capital of Yamanashi Prefecture, and the surrounding area is known for its vineyards.

▶ Fuji-go-ko is a mountain and lake resort area at the foot of Mt. Fuji.

第6章

中部

7 長野県

▶ 長野県は、日本アルプスの最高峰の山々が位置するところです。

▶ 長野はウィンタースポーツを楽しむのに最適で、1998年には冬季オリンピックも開催されました。

▶ 長野は昔は信濃と呼ばれ、今でもこの呼び方が使われることがよくあります。

▶ 長野県の県庁所在地は長野市で、642年に善光寺が建立されたことから発展しました。

▶ 松本は城下町で、長野の主要都市のうちのひとつです。

▶ 木曽は長野の山間の谷に位置し、封建時代からの古い宿場町が点在しています。

Nagano

▶ Nagano Prefecture is the area where many of the highest mountains of the Japan Alps can be found.

▶ Nagano is also a good place to enjoy winter sports, and the Winter Olympics were held there in 1998.

▶ Nagano was once called Shinano, and that name is still used on many occasions.

▶ Nagano City is the capital of Nagano Prefecture, and it began to develop when Zenko-ji Temple was erected there in 642.

▶ Matsumoto is a castle town and one of the major cities of Nagano.

▶ The Kiso district is a mountain valley in Nagano, and there are some cozy post-station towns from the feudal period there.

第6章

中部

8 新潟県

▶ 新潟県は、日本海に面し、ロシア東部からの
入口になっています。

▶ 新潟市は新潟県の県庁所在地で、東京から上
越新幹線を使えば簡単に行けます。

▶ 長岡と新潟県の山沿いで、世界最深積雪を記
録しました。

▶ 佐渡は日本海に浮かぶ島で、かつては金山が
あることで知られていました。

Niigata

▶ Niigata Prefecture faces the Sea of Japan and is a gateway to eastern Russia.

▶ Niigata City is the capital of Niigata Prefecture and can be accessed easily using the Joetsu Shinkansen from Tokyo.

▶ Nagaoka and the mountain-side of Niigata Prefecture set records for some of the deepest snow accumulations in the world.

▶ Sado is an island in the Sea of Japan and was once known for its gold mines.

9 富山県

▶ 富山は富山県の県庁所在地で、日本海の富山湾に面しています。

▶ 立山連峰は、登山のほかにスキーリゾートとしても知られています。

▶ 富山周辺はイカやカニなどの海産物が豊富です。

▶ 富山の山間には昔ながらの集落が残っています。五箇山もそのひとつで、世界遺産に登録されています。

Toyama

▶ Toyama is the capital of Toyama Prefecture and faces Toyama Bay on the Sea of Japan.

▶ The Tateyama Mountains are well known for ski resorts as well as mountaineering.

▶ The Toyama area produces seafood such as squid and crab.

▶ There are some historical villages found in the mountain area of Toyama. Gokayama is one of them, and it is designated as a World Heritage Site.

第6章

中部

10 石川県

▶ 金沢は北陸地方にある町で、日本庭園で知られる兼六園や武家屋敷など、史跡がたくさんあります。

▶ 金沢は、江戸時代に権勢を振るった前田家が統治していた歴史的な町です。

▶ 金沢では洗練された見事な工芸品を見ることができます。そのひとつが日本の焼き物のひとつである九谷焼です。

▶ 加賀友禅と呼ばれる染め物は、金沢の工芸品として有名です。

▶ 輪島とその周辺は、ひなびた村々や、民芸品、そして美しい海岸線で知られています。

Ishikawa

▶ Kanazawa is a city in the Hokuriku area and is home to many historic sites, such as the famous Kenroku-en traditional Japanese garden and an old samurai district.

▶ Kanazawa is a historical city once ruled by the Maeda clan, one of the most powerful families of the Edo period.

▶ You can enjoy exquisite traditional crafts in Kanazawa. One of them is Kutani-yaki, a style of Japanese porcelain.

▶ Dyed fabrics called Kaga yuzen are also famous crafts of Kanazawa.

▶ Wajima and its vicinity is famous for its cosy villages, local crafts, and beautiful coast lines.

福井県

▶ 福井県は京都の北に位置し、県庁所在地の福井市は城下町です。

▶ 福井県の県庁所在地の福井市の近くには、禅宗の一派である曹洞宗の大本山である永平寺があります。

▶ 福井は、東尋坊という岩だらけの細く伸びた海岸で有名です。

Fukui

▶ Fukui Prefecture is located north of Kyoto, and its capital is Fukui City, an old castletown.

▶ Near Fukui City, the capital of Fukui Prefecture, there is a temple called Eihei-ji that is the headquarters of the Soto-shu, one of the major Zen branches.

▶ Fukui is also famous for its long, rocky coast called Tojinbo.

第6章

中部

12 岐阜県

▶ 長野と同様に、岐阜県も内陸の山地をまたぐようにして広がっています。

▶ 岐阜県の白川郷は、茅葺きの急傾斜の屋根が特徴の家があることで知られており、世界遺産にも登録されています。

▶ 飛騨谷は、岐阜県の山間地方で、高山市はこの谷に古くからある町です。

Gifu

▶ Gifu Prefecture, like Nagano, stretches across the inland mountain area.

▶ Shirakawa Village in Gifu Prefecture is famous for its unique houses with thatched peaked roves, and it is designated as a World Heritage Site.

▶ The Hida Valley is a mountainous area in Gifu Prefecture, and Takayama-City is an old city in this valley.

13 愛知県

▶ 中部地方の中心は名古屋です。名古屋とその周辺で、日本第3の経済圏を形成しています。

▶ 名古屋は愛知県にあり、かつて尾張と呼ばれていました。

▶ 江戸時代の尾張は、将軍に最も近い親戚によって治められていました。

▶ 名古屋までは、東京から新幹線で1時間半で行けます。

Aichi

▶ The regional capital of the Chubu Region is Nagoya. Nagoya and its vicinity is the third-largest commercial area in Japan.

▶ Nagoya is in Aichi Prefecture and was once called Owari.

▶ Owari was governed by one of the most important relatives of the shogun during the Edo period.

▶ Nagoya can be reached by Shinkansen from Tokyo in one hour and thirty minutes.

第6章

中部

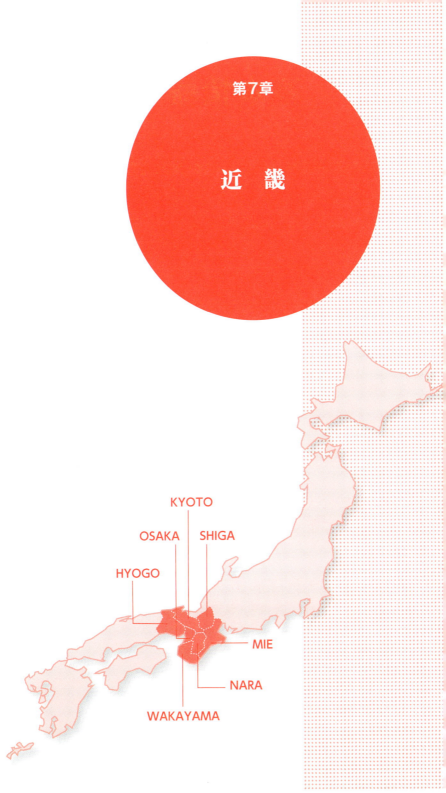

第7章

近畿

KYOTO

OSAKA

SHIGA

HYOGO

MIE

NARA

WAKAYAMA

1 基本情報

▶ 京都が位置しているのが近畿地方です。

▶ 近畿地方は、かつては日本の政治と文化の中心でした。

▶ 近畿地方最大の都市は大阪です。

▶ 大阪とその周辺地域は、東京に次いで、日本で2番目に大きい商業地区です。

▶ 京都は大阪の東に位置しており、通勤列車で簡単に行くことができます。

▶ 近畿地方には4つの県と、2つの「府」という特別の行政区があります。

Basic Tips

▶ The Kinki Region is the place where Kyoto is located.

▶ The Kinki Region was once the nation's political and cultural center.

▶ The biggest city in the Kinki Region is Osaka.

▶ Osaka and its vicinity is the second-largest commercial area in Japan, after Tokyo.

▶ Kyoto is located east of Osaka and is easily accessed by commuter trains.

▶ There are four prefectures and two special prefectures called "*fu*" in the Kinki Region.

第7章

近畿

2 自然

▶ 紀伊半島という大きな半島には、深い山や谷があり、その美しい海岸線も楽しむことができます。

▶ 名古屋の西から、南方向へ伸びる紀伊半島から、日本の多くの古代史が始まりました。

▶ 紀伊半島にはいくつかとても重要な神社や寺があります。こうした場所を結ぶ巡礼の道を熊野古道と言います。

3 伊勢神宮

▶ 紀伊半島の東側には伊勢神宮という神社があります。

Nature

▶ There is a large peninsula called the Kii-hanto where you can enjoy deep mountain forests and valleys, and a scenic coastline.

▶ The Kii Peninsula, which stretches southeward from the western area of Nagoya, is the place where almost all of Japan's ancient history was drawn from.

▶ There are several important shrines and temples on the Kii Peninsula. The pilgrimage route connecting such places is called the Kumano Kodo.

Ise-jingu

▶ On the eastern side of the Kii Peninsula there is a Shinto shrine called Ise-jingu.

▶ 伊勢神宮は皇室にとっての氏神で、日本で最も崇拝される神社の一つです。

▶ 伊勢神宮は約 2000 年前に建てられました。

大和

▶ 紀伊半島の中央部を大和と呼び、そこは古代の朝廷があったところです。

▶ 大和地方は日本の国が誕生したところとされています。

▶ 大和地方には、1500 年以上前の古墳、寺、神社などが多く残っています。

▶ Ise-jingu is a shrine for the emperor, and it is one of the most revered in the country.

▶ Ise-jingu was erected around 2,000 years ago.

Yamato

▶ The center portion of the Kii Peninsula is called Yamato, and it is where the sites of ancient imperial courts were found.

▶ The Yamato area is considered the birthplace of the Japanese nation.

▶ In the Yamato area, you will find countless ancient tombs, temples, and shrines from more than 1,500 years ago.

5 交通

▶ 近畿地方を訪れるには、新幹線が便利です。

▶ 直接近畿地方に入りたい人には、関西国際空港が玄関口となっています。

▶ 近鉄（電車）は奈良、大和、伊勢間を効率よく結んでいます。

▶ 近鉄（電車）はネットワークが便利な私鉄線です。

Transportation

▶ The Shinkansen is a convenient way to visit the Kinki Region.

▶ Kansai International Airport is the gateway for people who want to visit the Kinki Region directly.

▶ The Kintetsu Railway has an excellent rail network for visiting Nara, Yamato, and Ise.

▶ The Kintetsu Railway is known for its convenient private railway networks.

第
7
章

近
畿

6 大阪府

▶ 大阪は大阪府とよばれる特別区で、日本で2番目に大きい経済の中心地です。

▶ 大阪は長らく日本の文化の中心地であった京都に近く、また西日本最大の都市として発展したため、独自の文化を築いてきました。

▶ 全国からあらゆる食材が集まる「天下の台所」であり、瀬戸内の海産物や大阪近郊の野菜にも恵まれ、日本料理の基礎となった食文化が栄え、「大阪の食い倒れ」という諺まで生まれました。

▶ 庶民の娯楽として、上方落語、漫才、吉本新喜劇・松竹新喜劇などのお笑い文化が栄えています。

Osaka

▶ Osaka is a special prefecture called Osaka-fu, and it is Japan's second-largest industrial and economic center.

▶ Situated near Kyoto, the time-honored center of Japanese culture, as well as being the largest city in western Japan, Osaka has developed its own unique culture.

▶ Foodstuffs from around the nation find their way to Osaka, which is the reason it is called the nation's kitchen. It is blessed by the marine products from the Inland Sea and by vegetables from the Osaka suburbs, enabling it to establish the foundations of Japanese cuisine culture. Osakans are so fond of eating that, according to an old adage, they constantly run the risk of eating themselves into penury.

▶ Popular culture is characterized by the comedic entertainment of *rakugo, manzai*, and Yoshimoto and Shochiku Shinkigeki theater.

第7章

近畿

7 京都府

▶ 京都は京都府とよばれる特別区で、京都市が県庁所在地です。

▶ 京都府は京都市だけではなく、景観の美しい若狭湾岸までの北部も含みます。

▶ 京都府の北には、深い杉の森林が広がっています。

Kyoto

▶ Kyoto is a special prefecture called Kyoto-fu, and its capital is Kyoto city.

▶ Kyoto-fu is not only the city of Kyoto but also covers the northern area between the city up to the scenic coast of Wakasa Bay.

▶ There is deep cedar forest stretching into the northern part of Kyoto-fu.

8 奈良県

▶ 奈良県は紀伊半島の真ん中あたりに位置し、奈良市が県庁所在地です。

▶ 奈良は日本でも指折りの歴史の町で、710年から792年の間、都が置かれていたところです。

▶ 奈良は京都から簡単に行けます。電車で京都駅から30分ほどです。

▶ 京都と比べると、奈良はかなりリラックスした雰囲気です。

Nara

▶ Nara Prefecture is located at the center of the Kii Peninsula, and the capital is Nara City.

▶ Nara is the most famous ancient city in Japan, and the capital was located there between 710 and 792.

▶ Nara can be visited from Kyoto easily. It is only 30 minutes from Kyoto Station by train.

▶ Compared with Kyoto, the atmosphere of Nara is quite relaxed.

第7章

近畿

▶ 東大寺は、752 年に完成した世界最大の銅製の大仏で有名です。

▶ 奈良西部には、680 年に建立された薬師寺があります。

▶ 薬師寺は美しい三重塔が有名で、これは 730 年に建てられたものです。

▶ 法隆寺は世界で最も古い木造建築で、607 年に完成しました。

▶ 奈良地方にある東大寺、薬師寺、法隆寺など多くの寺には、中国文化の影響が強く見られます。

▶ Todai-ji Temple is famous for having the world's largest bronze Buddha statue, which was completed in 752.

▶ In the western area of Nara, you will find Yakushi-ji Temple, which was erected in 680.

▶ Yakushi-ji Temple is famous for its beautiful three-story pagoda, which was erected in 730.

▶ Horyu-ji Temple is the oldest wooden structure in the world. It was completed in 607.

▶ In many temples, such as Todai-ji, Yakushi-ji, and Horyu-ji, around the Nara area, you will find a strong influence from ancient Chinese culture.

9 和歌山県

▶ 和歌山県は紀伊半島の西に位置し、和歌山市が県庁所在地です。

▶ 和歌山の南部は太平洋に面しており、温暖な気候で知られています。

▶ 和歌山県には高野山という山があり、そこは日本の密教である真言宗の総本山です。

Wakayama

▶ Wakayama Prefecture is located on the western side of the Kii Peninsula, and Wakayama City is its capital.

▶ The southern part of Wakayama faces the Pacific Ocean, and it is known for its warm weather.

▶ In Wakayama Prefecture, there is a mountain called Koya-san, which is the headquarters of Shingon-shu, a famous esoteric Buddhist sect in Japan.

第7章

近畿

10 三重県

▶ 三重県は奈良県の東に位置し、名古屋にも近いです。県庁所在地は津市です。

▶ 三重県の東海岸にある伊勢志摩地方は、神道でも最も神聖な場所として知られています。伊勢神宮もここにあります。

▶ 伊勢志摩の海岸に沿って、たくさんの真珠養殖場があります。

Mie

▶ Mie Prefecture is located east of Nara Prefecture and is close to Nagoya. Its capital is Tsu City.

▶ The area of Ise-Shima is on the eastern coast of Mie and is known as one of Shinto's most sacred places. Ise Shrine is also located there.

▶ There are many pearl fisheries along the scenic coast of Ise-Shima.

第7章

近畿

11 兵庫県

▶ 兵庫県は大阪の西に位置しています。

▶ 神戸は兵庫県の県庁所在地で、日本で最も重要な港町のひとつです。

▶ 淡路島は瀬戸内海で最大の島で、本州とは明石海峡大橋でつながっています。

▶ 淡路島は大鳴門橋で、四国の徳島ともつながっています。

▶ 明石海峡大橋は，世界最長の吊り橋です。

▶ 姫路は姫路城という美しいお城があることで知られています。姫路城は 1993 年に世界遺産に登録されています。

Hyogo

▶ Hyogo Prefecture is west of Osaka.

▶ Kobe is the capital of Hyogo and is known as one of the most important port towns in Japan.

▶ Awaji-shima is the biggest island in the Seto Naikai, or Seto Inland Sea, and it is connected to the mainland by the Akashi Kaikyo Bridge.

▶ Awaji-shima Island is also connected to Tokushima in Shikoku by the Onaruto Bridge.

▶ The Akashi Kaikyo Bridge is the longest suspension bridge in the world.

▶ Himeji is a city which is famous for its beautiful castle called Himeji-jo, which was designated as a World Heritage Site in 1993.

第7章

近畿

12 滋賀県

▶ 滋賀県は日本最大の湖、琵琶湖があることで有名です。

▶ 滋賀県の県庁所在地は大津市で、京都まで電車でわずか10分の距離です。

▶ 世界遺産である比叡山延暦寺をはじめとする多数の寺院や史跡があります。

Shiga

▶ Shiga prefecture is famous for Japan's largest lake, Lake Biwa.

▶ The capital of Shiga prefecture is situated in Otsu city, only ten minutes by train from Kyoto.

▶ Shiga prefecture is the location of many famous temples and historical sites, including the World Heritage Site Enryaku-ji on Mount Hiei.

第7章

近畿

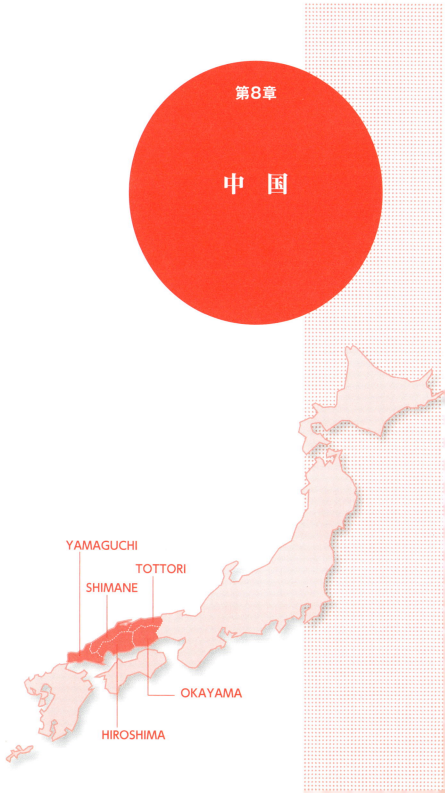

第8章

中 国

YAMAGUCHI

TOTTORI

SHIMANE

OKAYAMA

HIROSHIMA

1 基本情報

▶ 中国地方は本州の西の地域です。

▶ 中国地方は瀬戸内海という内海にそって広がっています。

▶ 中国地方には5つの県があります。

▶ 中国地方で一番大きい都市は広島市です。

2 交通

▶ 瀬戸内海に面した側を山陽と言います。

▶ 山陽の主な都市には、新幹線で行くことができます。

Basic Tips

▶ The Chugoku Region is in western Honshu.

▶ The Chugoku Region stretches along an inland sea called the Seto Naikai.

▶ There are five prefectures in the Chugoku Region.

▶ The biggest city in the Chugoku Region is Hiroshima.

Transportation

▶ The area facing the Seto Naikai is called San'yo.

▶ Major cities of the San'yo area are linked by Shinkansen.

第8章

中
国

▶ 東京から広島までは、新幹線で4時間半です。

 瀬戸内海

▷ 瀬戸内海は本州と四国の間にあります。

▷ 瀬戸内海は重要な海の交通ルートであるだけ
でなく、小さな島が点在する景観の美しいと
ころです。

▷ 瀬戸内海は本州と四国を隔てていますが、橋
で行き来できます。

 広島と原爆

▷ 広島は、1945年に原爆で破壊されたことから、
世界中で知られています。

▶ From Tokyo to Hiroshima, it takes four hours and thirty minutes by Shinkansen.

Seto Inland Sea

▶ The Seto Naikai, or Seto Inland Sea, separates Honshu from Shikoku.

▶ The Seto Naikai, or Seto Inland Sea, is not only an important ocean transportation route but also a scenic area dotted with small islands.

▶ The Seto Naikai, or Seto Inland Sea, separates Honshu from Shikoku, and there are bridges connecting these two regions.

Hiroshima and the Atom Bomb

▶ Hiroshima is known around the world because it was destroyed by an atomic bomb in 1945.

第8章

中国

▶ 1945 年 8 月 6 日、原爆が広島上空で爆発し、およそ 9 万人が即死しました。

▶ 広島では多くの人が放射能による健康被害に苦しみました。

▶ 20 万人以上の人が広島の原爆で亡くなりました。

▶ 第二次世界大戦後、広島は平和都市となりました。

▶ On August 6, 1945, an atomic bomb was exploded above Hiroshima, killing about 90,000 people instantly.

▶ Many people have suffered from diseases caused by radiation in Hiroshima.

▶ More than 200,000 people were killed by the atomic bomb in Hiroshima.

▶ After the Second World War, Hiroshima became a city dedicated to peace.

5 鳥取県

▶ 鳥取県は日本海に面し、県庁所在地は鳥取市です。

▶ 鳥取市の海岸には、鳥取砂丘という大きな砂丘があります。

▶ 米子近辺は、鳥取県の産業の中心です。

▶ 47 都道府県中、最も人口が少ない県です。総人口は約 57 万人です。

Tottori

▶ Tottori Prefecture faces the Sea of Japan, and its capital is Tottori City.

▶ Near the seashore in Tottori City, there is a large sand dune called the Tottori-sakyu.

▶ The Yonago area is an industrial center in Tottori Prefecture.

▶ Among the 47 Japanese administrative divisions, Tottori prefecture is the least populous, being inhabited by some 570,000 people.

第8章

中国

6 島根県

▶ 島根県は日本海に面し、鳥取県の西に位置します。

▶ 松江は島根県の県庁所在地で、城下町として知られています。

▶ 出雲には出雲大社という重要な神社があり、ここは日本神話の時代まで遡ることができます。

▶ 離島の隠岐島、竹島も島根県に含まれます。

Shimane

▶ Shimane Prefecture faces the Sea of Japan and is located west of Tottori Prefecture.

▶ Matsue is the capital of Shimane Prefecture and is famous as a castle town.

▶ Izumo is known for a major Shinto shrine called Izumo Taisha that probably dates back to the era of legend when Japan was established.

▶ The isolated islands of Oki and Takeshima fall within the prefecture's boundaries.

第8章

中国

7 岡山県

▶ 岡山県は広島の東に位置し、県庁所在地は岡山市です。

▶ 岡山県の南部は、小さな島が点在する瀬戸内海に面しています。

▶ 日本3名園の1つである後楽園という日本庭園が有名です。

▶ 岡山の南部に位置する倉敷市は、川沿いの白壁の街並みが美しく、観光地として人気があります。

Okayama

▶ Okayama Prefecture is east of Hiroshima, and its capital is Okayama City.

▶ The south part of Okayama Prefecture faces the Seto Naikai, which is dotted with small islands.

▶ Okayama's Koraku-en is widely known as one of the Three Great Gardens of Japan.

▶ Kurashiki city, located in the southern part of the prefecture, is popular among tourists for its beautiful urban riverscape and white-walled storehouses.

第8章

中国

8 広島県

▶ 広島県は、山口県と岡山県に挟まれ、県庁所在地は広島市です。

▶ 今では広島は、この地方の商業・産業の中心地で、100万人以上の人が住んでいます。

▶ 宮島と原爆ドームの2つの世界遺産を有し、海外からの観光客が増えています。

Hiroshima

▶ Hiroshima Prefecture is located between Yamaguchi and Okayama prefectures, and its capital is Hiroshima City.

▶ Now Hiroshima is the commercial and industrial center of this region, and there are more than one million people living there.

▶ The temple complex of Itsukushima and the A-bomb Dome are designated World Heritage Sites and draw a growing number of tourists from abroad.

第8章

中国

山口県

▶ 山口県は本州の西の端に位置し、九州とは関門橋で結ばれています。

▶ 山口県はかつて封建時代には長州と呼ばれ、明治維新をもたらすのに重要な役割を果たした大藩でした。

▶ 萩は長州の昔の都で、興味深い史跡がたくさんあります。

▶ 山口県の下関は、中国地方の西の端に位置し、関門海峡を挟んで、九州と対峙しています。

Yamaguchi

▶ Yamaguchi Prefecture is located at the western end of Honshu and is connected to Kyushu by the Kanmon-kyo Bridge.

▶ Yamaguchi Prefecture was called Choshu during the feudal period and was a powerful feudal domain that took an important role in bringing about the Meiji Restoration.

▶ Hagi was the old capital of Choshu, and you can visit many interesting historical sites there.

▶ Shimonoseki in Yamaguchi Prefecture is the westernmost city in Chugoku and faces Kyushu across the Kanmon Kaikyo, or Kanmon Straits.

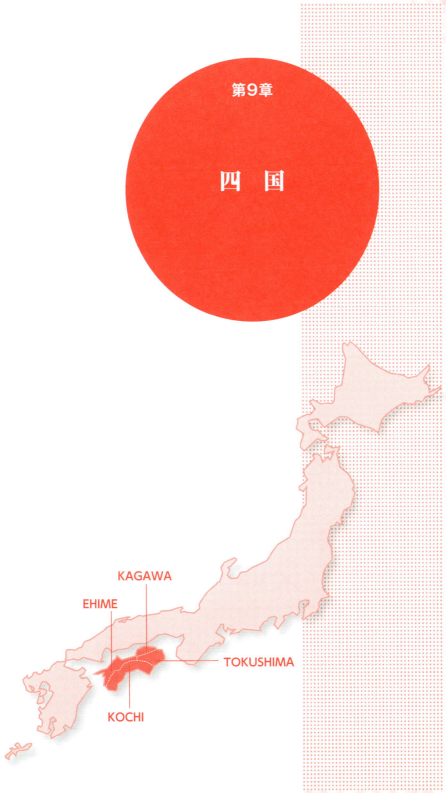

第9章

四 国

KAGAWA

EHIME

TOKUSHIMA

KOCHI

1 基本情報

▶ 四国は、中国地方の南、瀬戸内海を渡ったところに位置しています。

▶ 四国には4つ県があり、すべての県が海と接しています。

▶ 四国は本州四国連絡橋という橋で行き来することができます。

▶ 四国はミカンと海産物が有名です。

2 交通

▶ 中国地方の岡山から、瀬戸内海を渡る列車で四国に行くことができます。

Basic Tips

▶ Shikoku is located south of the Chugoku Region across an inland sea called the Seto Naikai.

▶ Shikoku is made up of four prefectures, and all its prefectures touch the sea.

▶ Shikoku is connected with Honshu by several bridges called the Honshu Shikoku Renraku-kyo.

▶ Shikoku is famous for its oranges and seafood.

Transportation

▶ From Okayama in the Chugoku Region, you can visit Shikoku via a train which crosses the Seto Naikai.

第9章

四国

▶ 四国に行くには、多くの人が新幹線で岡山まで行き、四国行きの電車に乗り換えます。

....

▶ 四国のすべての県庁所在地の近くには空港があり、東京や大阪から飛行機で行けます。

3 空海とお遍路

▶ 空海は昔の僧で、四国で生まれ、日本でも最も影響のある密教のひとつ、真言宗を開きました。

....

▶ 四国は、空海ゆかりの地 88 カ所のお寺を回る四国お遍路という巡礼で有名です。

....

▶ 四国 88 カ所を周る巡礼者のことを、日本語でお遍路さんと呼びます。

....

▶ お遍路は、日本人に人気の巡礼の旅で、全長 1200 キロ以上あります。

▶ To visit Shikoku, many people go to Okayama by Shinkansen and change to a train serving the Shikoku area.

▶ There are airports near all the prefectural capitals of Shikoku, connecting them with Tokyo and Osaka.

Kukai and Pilgrimage

▶ Kukai was an ancient monk who was born in Shikoku and founded the Shingon-shu, one of the most influential esoteric Buddhist sects in Japan.

▶ Shikoku is known for the Shikoku Henro, or pilgrimage of 88 temples associated with a famous priest called Kukai.

▶ Pilgrims who are visiting the 88 temples in Shikoku are called *ohenro-san* in Japanese.

▶ *Ohenro* is a popular pilgrimage among Japanese people, and its length is more than 1,200 kilometers.

第9章

四国

 **愛媛県**

▶ 愛媛県は、四国の北西に位置し、県庁所在地は松山です。

▶ 松山は四国で最大の都市です。

▶ 道後は、松山市にほど近い温泉地として有名です。

▶ 石鎚山は、西日本で最も高い山で、仏教の修行の場として有名です。

Ehime

▶ Ehime Prefecture is in the northwest area of Shikoku, and its capital is Matsuyama.

▶ Matsuyama is the biggest city in Shikoku.

▶ Dogo is a famous hot-spring resort area close to the city of Matsuyama.

▶ Mt. Ishizuchi is the highest mountain in western Japan and is known as a place for Buddhist ascetic training.

第9章

四国

5 香川県

▶ 香川県は四国の北東に位置し、県庁所在地は高松です。

▶ 高松は、岡山との間の本州四国連絡橋を列車が通るようになり、とても便利になりました。

▶ 香川県は、讃岐うどんと呼ばれる麺で有名です。

Kagawa

▶ Kagawa Prefecture is located in the northeast part of Shikoku, and its capital is Takamatsu.

▶ Takamatsu became quite convenient after train service over the Honshi Renraku-kyo bridge from Okayama started.

▶ Kagawa Prefecture is famous for its noodles, which are called *Sanuki udon*.

第9章

四国

6 徳島県

▶ 徳島県は四国東部に位置し、県庁所在地は徳島です。

▶ 徳島市までは、瀬戸内海を渡る大きな吊橋を使うと、大阪や神戸から車で簡単に行けます。

▶ 鳴門海峡は、速い渦潮で有名です。

Tokushima

▶ Tokushima Prefecture is located on the east side of Shikoku, and its capital city is Tokushima.

▶ Tokushima City is easily accessed by car from Osaka and Kobe using the huge suspension bridges crossing the inland sea.

▶ The Naruto Strait is known for its fast, swirling current.

第9章

四国

7 高知県

▶ 高知県は四国の南側で、県庁所在地は高知市です。

▶ 高知県は太平洋に面し、黒潮と呼ばれる海流のおかげで温暖です。

▶ 高知はかつて土佐と呼ばれ、封建時代には山内氏が統治していました。

▶ 高知では、カツオやマグロなどの海の幸を楽しめます。

▶ 気候が温暖なので、高知では年に2度、米が収穫できます。

Kochi

▶ Kochi Prefecture is in the southern portion of Shikoku, and its capital is Kochi City.

▶ Kochi Prefecture faces the Pacific Ocean and is warmed by a current called the *Kuroshio*.

▶ Kochi was once called Tosa, and it was governed by the Yamanouchi clan during the feudal period.

▶ In Kochi, people enjoy seafood, including bonito and tuna.

▶ Thanks to the mild weather, rice can be harvested twice a year in Kochi.

第9章

四国

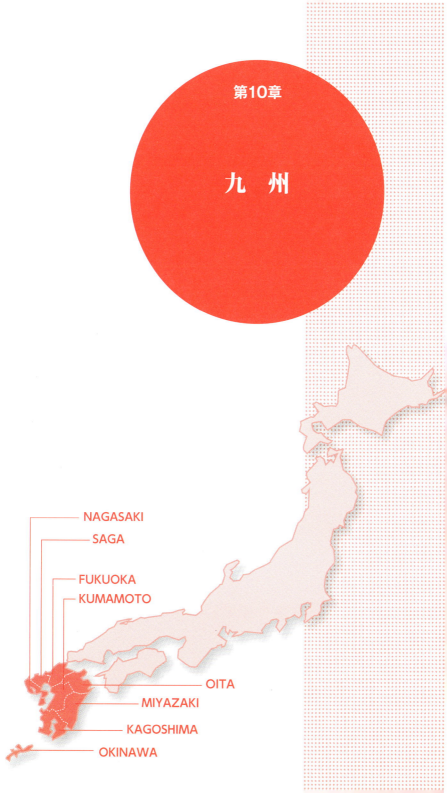

第10章

九　州

NAGASAKI

SAGA

FUKUOKA

KUMAMOTO

OITA

MIYAZAKI

KAGOSHIMA

OKINAWA

1 基本情報

▶ 九州は日本の主要4島のうち、最も南に位置しています。

▶ 九州は冬は暖かく、夏は暑いです。

▶ 九州地方の商業の中心は福岡市です。

▶ 九州と本州の間には関門海峡があります。

▶ 九州には多くの火山、温泉があり、美しい景観の海岸線も楽しめます。

▶ 九州には沖縄も含め8つの県があります。

Basic Tips

▶ Kyusyu is the southernmost of Japan's major four islands.

▶ Kyushu is mild in winter and quite hot in summer.

▶ The regional capital and commercial center of Kyushu is Fukuoka City.

▶ Kyushu is separated from Honshu by the Kanmon Strait.

▶ There are many volcanoes and hot springs in Kyushu, where people can also enjoy scenic coastlines.

▶ In Kyushu, there are eight prefectures, including Okinawa.

第10章

九州

2 交通

▶ 九州には東京から新幹線で行けます。所要時間は約5時間です。

▶ 東京から九州までは飛行機で1時間半かかります。

▶ 九州はアジアに近いので、何世紀もの間、日本への玄関口となってきました。

▶ とくに古代において、中国や韓国からの無数の技術、文化が、九州経由で、日本に入ってきました。

3 歴史

▶ 九州が、日本史の起源と考える人も多いです。

Transportasion

▶ You can visit Kyushu directly from Tokyo by Shinkansen. It takes about five hours.

▶ It takes one hour and thirty minutes to fly from Tokyo to Kyushu.

▶ Because it is near the Asian continent, Kyushu has been the primary gateway to Japan for many centuries.

▶ Particularly in ancient times, countless technologies and waves of culture came from China and Korea to Japan via Kyushu.

History

▶ Many believe that Kyushu is the birthplace of Japanese history.

第10章

九州

▶ 九州には、先史時代からの考古学的な遺跡が無数にあります。

▶ 日本が江戸時代に鎖国をしている間、長崎の出島と呼ばれる人工島が唯一の開かれた港で、オランダ商人のみここで貿易することができました。

4 隠れキリシタン

▶ 九州西部はその昔、キリスト教が幕府によって禁止されていたとき、隠れキリシタンがいたところとして知られています。

▶ 幕府によってキリスト教が禁止されていた頃、隠れてキリスト教を信仰していた人を、隠れキリシタンといいます。

▶ 多くの隠れキリシタンが、17世紀、長崎県や熊本県で殉教しました。

▶ There are countless archeological sites from the prehistoric era in Kyushu.

▶ While Japan was secluded in the Edo period, an artificial island called Dejima in Nagasaki was the only port that was open, and only Dutch merchants could trade there.

Underground Christian Believers

▶ Western Kyushu is known for its secret underground activity when Christianity was strictly banned by the shogunate.

▶ The underground Christian believers were called *Kakure Kirishitan* when Christianity was strictly banned by the shogunate.

▶ Many underground Christian believers were martyred in the seventeenth century in the current Nagasaki and Kumamoto prefectures.

第10章

九州

5 福岡県

▶ 福岡県は九州の北端に位置し、県庁所在地は福岡市です。

▶ 福岡は九州の商業の中心です。

▶ 福岡空港からは、アジア各地へ飛行機で行くことができます。

▶ 福岡と韓国の釜山の間には、ホバークラフトが運行しています。

▶ 博多山笠は、勢いのいい元気な祭りとして知られています。装飾の施された山車を担ぎ、通りに勢いよく出ていきます。

▶ 北九州市はかつて鉄鋼業で栄えましたが、それは炭鉱が町の南部にあったおかげです。

Fukuoka

▶ Fukuoka Prefecture is located in the northernmost part of Kyushu, and its capital is Fukuoka City.

▶ Fukuoka is the commercial center of Kyushu.

▶ From Fukuoka Airport, you can fly to many Asian countries.

▶ There is a hovercraft service between Fukuoka and Busan in Korea.

▶ *Hakata Yamagasa* is known for its lively and vivid festival. People carry decorated floats and rush through the streets.

▶ Kitakyushu City once prospered thanks to its steel industry, which was supported by coal mines located south of the city.

第10章

九州

6 佐賀県

▶ 佐賀は、福岡県と長崎県に挟まれた県です。県庁所在地は佐賀市です。

▶ 佐賀は伝統的な陶器で有名です。伊万里、唐津、有田市などでたくさんの陶器が作られています。

▶ 佐賀南部は有明海に面しています。湾の干潟にはムツゴロウというひょうきんな魚が生息します。

▶ 佐賀県北部では、リアス式海岸にそって素晴らしい景色が堪能できます。

Saga

▶ Saga is the prefecture located between Fukuoka and Nagasaki prefectures. Its capital is Saga City.

▶ Saga is famous for its traditional ceramic art. There is a lot of pottery produced in the cities of Imari, Karatsu, and Arita.

▶ The southern part of Saga faces a bay called the Ariake-kai. It is known for cute fish called *mutsugoro* living on the tidelands of the bay.

▶ In the northern part of Saga Prefecture, people can enjoy scenic views along the sawtooth coastline.

第10章

九州

7 長崎県

▶ 長崎は九州の西の端に位置しています。

▶ 長崎は 1945 年に 2 発目の原爆が落とされた町です。

▶ 広島と同様、長崎も平和都市になりました。

▶ 封建時代、長崎は日本において海外に開かれた唯一の窓でした。

▶ チャンポンは長崎に住む中国人が作り出した麺料理です。

▶ 長崎県の西岸に沿っては、数えきれない島や入り江があります。

▶ 島原半島には雲仙岳という火山があります。島原市はこの半島にある美しい城下町です。

Nagasaki

▶ Nagasaki is located at the western end of Kyushu.

▶ Nagasaki is known for being the city where the second atomic bomb was dropped in 1945.

▶ Like Hiroshima, Nagasaki became a city dedicated to peace.

▶ In the feudal period, Nagasaki was the only window Japan had to the world.

▶ *Chanpon* is a noodle dish invented by Chinese people living in Nagasaki.

▶ Along the western coastline of Nagasaki Prefecture, you can see countless islands and coves.

▶ There is a volcano called Unzen-dake on the Shimabara Peninsula. Shimabara City is located on this peninsula and is a beautiful castle town.

第10章

九州

8 熊本県

▶ 熊本は福岡の南にある県で、県庁所在地は熊本市です。熊本市は熊本城で有名です。

▶ 阿蘇山は熊本県にある火山で、九州の中央に位置しています。

▶ 熊本県西岸には、天草諸島という景色のよい島々が点在しています。

Kumamoto

▶ Kumamoto is a prefecture located south of Fukuoka, and its capital is Kumamoto City. Kumamoto City is famous for its castle.

▶ Mt. Aso in Kumamoto Prefecture is a volcano located in the center of Kyushu.

▶ There are scenic islands called the Amakusa Islands, which dot the Western coast of Kumamoto Prefecture.

9 大分県

▶ 大分県は熊本県の東に位置し、山やリアス式海岸が見事な景観を作り出しています。県庁所在地は大分市です。

▶ 大分県の別府と湯布院は、温泉地として有名で、その他、山間部にもたくさんの温泉があります。

▶ 国東半島の谷あいにはたくさんの仏教寺院があり、修行の場として知られています。

▶ 大分県の宇佐という街には宇佐八幡宮があり、そこは武人の守り神とされています。

Oita

▶ Oita Prefecture is located east of Kumamoto and is quite scenic because of its mountains and sawtooth coastline. Its capital is Oita City.

▶ Beppu and Yufuin in Oita Prefecture are famous hot-spring resorts, and there are many other hot-spring villages in the mountainous areas.

▶ There are many Buddhist temples in the valleys of the Kunisaki Peninsula, which are known as training centers for Buddhist ascetics.

▶ Usa is a town in Oita Prefecture where Usa Hachiman-gu, a shrine dedicated to the tutelary god of warriors, is located.

第10章

九州

10 宮崎県

▶ 宮崎県は九州の南東にあり、黒潮が流れているため気候はとても温暖です。県庁所在地は宮崎市です。

▶ 高千穂は、日本統治のためにニニギノミコトが降臨した場所と言われています。

▶ 日南海岸は太平洋に面した人気の観光地です。

Miyazaki

▶ Miyazaki Prefecture is in the southeast part of Kyushu, and its weather is quite mild because of the *Kuroshio* Current. Its capital is Miyazaki City.

▶ Takachiho is the village where the god Ninigi is said to have descended from Heaven to rule over the land.

▶ The Nichinan coast, which faces the Pacific Ocean, is a well-known resort area.

第10章

九州

11 鹿児島県

▶ 鹿児島県は九州の南部に位置し、県庁所在地は鹿児島市です。

▶ 鹿児島湾には桜島があり、活火山です。この火山は鹿児島市の向い側にあります。

▶ 鹿児島湾は大隅と薩摩の2つの半島に挟まれています。これらの半島はとても景色のいいところです。

▶ 封建時代、鹿児島は薩摩と呼ばれ、島津氏が統治する強力な藩でした。

▶ 鹿児島県には自然のすばらしい奄美諸島もあります。

▶ 種子島は、JAXA（宇宙航空研究開発機構）が運営する宇宙センターがあることで知られています。

Kagoshima

▶ Kagoshima Prefecture lies in the southern part of Kyushu, and its capital is Kagoshima City.

▶ In Kagoshima Bay, there is a mountain called Sakurajima, which is an active volcano. This volcano faces the city of Kagoshima.

▶ Kagoshima Bay is sandwiched between two peninsulas called Osumi and Satsuma. Both peninsulas are quite scenic.

▶ Kagoshima was called Satsuma and was a powerful feudal domain ruled by the Shimazu clan in the feudal period.

▶ Kagoshima Prefecture includes the beautiful Amami Islands.

▶ Tanegashima is known for its space center managed by JAXA, the Japan Aerospace Exploration Agency.

12 沖縄県

▶ 沖縄も九州の一部ですが、歴史的にも文化的にもまったく異なります。

▶ 沖縄は九州と台湾の間に位置しています。

▶ 沖縄県は、亜熱帯気候に属しています。

▶ 沖縄は、160の島が連なる南西諸島の南にあり、その県庁所在地は那覇です。

▶ 沖縄県の属する南西諸島を琉球諸島と呼びます。

▶ 沖縄の文化やライフスタイルは、その位置、歴史的背景により、ほかの日本の地域とはまったく異なっています。

Okinawa

▶ Okinawa is considered to be part of Kyushu, but it has a very different historical and cultural background.

▶ Okinawa is located between Kyushu and Taiwan.

▶ Okinawa Prefecture has a subtropical climate.

▶ Okinawa is in the southern portion of the Nansei island chain and consists of 160 islands. Its capital is Naha.

▶ The portion of the Nansei island chain belonging to Okinawa Prefecture is called the Ryukyu Islands.

▶ Because of its location and historical background, Okinawa's culture and lifestyles are quite different from rest of the nation's.

第10章

九州

▶ 島唄は沖縄の民謡で、地元の弦楽器である三線にあわせて歌われます。

▶ 三線は蛇皮線とも呼ばれます。三線は沖縄独特の楽器で、弦が3本で、胴の部分には蛇の皮が張られています。

▶ 尖閣諸島は沖縄本島の遠く南に浮かぶ島で、台湾にも近いです。

▶ 沖縄はかつては琉球王国という独立国でした。

▶ 那覇には、ユネスコの世界遺産に登録されている首里城という城があります。

▶ 沖縄が公式に日本となったのは1879年のことです。

▶ *Shima-uta* is Okinawa's folk music, and it is often played with the *sanshin*, a local stringed instrument.

▶ *Sanshin* are also called *jabisen*. The *sanshin* is Okinawa's local instrument, which consists of a snakeskin-covered body with three strings.

▶ The Senkaku Shoto are islands located far south of the main island of Okinawa, and are close to Taiwan.

▶ Okinawa was once an independent country called the Ryukyu Kingdom.

▶ In Naha, there is a palace called Shuri-jo Castle, which is a UNESCO World Heritage Site.

▶ Okinawa formally became a part of Japan in 1879.

▶ 1945 年、沖縄はアメリカ軍に攻撃され、激しい戦場となりました。

▶ 沖縄の戦闘で、9 万 4000 人以上の人が亡くなり、その多くが一般市民でした。

▶ 沖縄戦の被害者には看護師として従軍していた若い女学生もいました。彼女たちはひめゆり部隊として知られています。

▶ 沖縄は第二次世界大戦中、唯一アメリカ軍が侵攻した県です。

▶ 日米安全保障条約により、沖縄本島にはたくさんの米軍基地があります。

▶ 日本人にとって、沖縄本島の 18％を占める米軍基地の問題は、賛否両論ある政治的関心事です。

▶ In 1945, Okinawa was attacked by the United States and became a brutal battlefield.

▶ In the Battle of Okinawa, more than 94,000 people died, many of them civilians.

▶ Among the victims of the Battle of Okinawa were young female students who worked as nurses. They were known as the *Himeyuri Butai*.

▶ Okinawa is the only prefecture that was invaded by the United States military during the Second World War.

▶ Based on the Japan-US Security Treaty, there are many United States bases on the main island of Okinawa.

▶ For Japanese people, the issue of United States bases in Okinawa, which occupy 18 percent of Okinawa's main island, is a controversial political matter.

九州

English Conversational Ability Test
国際英語会話能力検定

● E-CATとは…

英語が話せるようになるための
テストです。インターネット
ベースで、30分であなたの発
話力をチェックします。

www.ecatexam.com

● iTEP®とは…

世界各国の企業、政府機関、アメリカの大学
300校以上が、英語能力判定テストとして採用。
オンラインによる90分のテストで文法、リー
ディング、リスニング、ライティング、スピー
キングの5技能をスコア化。iTEP®は、留学、就
職、海外赴任などに必要な、世界に通用する英
語力を総合的に評価する画期的なテストです。

www.itepexamjapan.com

30秒でできる！
47都道府県紹介
おもてなしの英会話

2017年2月7日　第1刷発行

監　修　　安河内 哲也

発行者　　浦　　晋 亮

発行所　　IBCパブリッシング株式会社
　　　　　〒162-0804 東京都新宿区中里町29番3号 菱秀神楽坂ビル9F
　　　　　Tel. 03-3513-4511　Fax. 03-3513-4512
　　　　　www.ibcpub.co.jp

印刷所　　中央精版印刷株式会社

ISBN978-4-7946-0459-0